WHY DO ROOS-
Crow Early in the Mo

A BOOK ABOUT FARM ANIMALS
Written by Jack Beard Illustrated by Jayri Gómez

T0179817

Have you ever wondered WHY farm animals do the things they do?

Farm animals are fun to see and even more fun to learn about. Each of these animals has something special that helps them live happily on the farm.

chicken

pig

pond

ducklings

ducks

Why do PIGS roll around in the MUD?

Why do PIGS roll around in the MUD?

fence

PIG SHAMPOO

PIG Conditioner

mud

PIG SPA

Are they enjoying a PIGGY SPA DAY?

cloud

carrots

apple

What color is the ball?

Why do DUCKS play in the RAIN?

Can you flap your arms like a duck?

rain

duck

mushroom

puddle

moon

star

Is it because they like to WIGGLE their tail feathers and FLAP their wings to the rhythm of the raindrops?

rain cloud
What color is the mushroom?
rain
ducklings
leaf
flower

Ducks love the rain, but they don't need rain boots and raincoats like you because their feathers keep them dry. Their bodies create a special oil that covers their feathers and makes them waterproof!

Are they trying to SHOW OFF their great singing voice to all the hens in the coop?

Roosters mainly crow to communicate. Sometimes it's to let the hens know it is time to wake up and start the day. Other times they want to let other roosters know who is boss. They even crow to alert the flock that danger is nearby.

roosters

chicks

Why do CHICKS have YELLOW feathers?
Is it so they can HIDE in the hay?

cracked egg

shell

Can you sing
the sleepy chick
a lullaby?

Chicks actually don't have feathers when they are born.
They have a layer of fuzzy down. If their down is white,
it gets stained yellow when they are inside their egg.
As the chicks grow, they lose their yellow down and grow
feathers instead.

hen

eggs

coop

Why do SHEEP have WOOL?

fence

sheep

flower

Can you find the sheep that is knitting?

Is it so they can make SWEATERS for other farm animals to keep them warm?

donkey

pig

cow

hen   chick

duck   ducklings

How many sheep can you count in the barn?

moon

star

tree

barn

Wool is a special type of coat that grows on sheep's bodies. It keeps the sheep warm and dry. Farmers cut off the wool from the sheep when the weather is warm to keep the sheep cool. This is called shearing. That wool can then turn into yarn that can be made into sweaters for us!

snowflake

Why do HORSES wear SHOES?

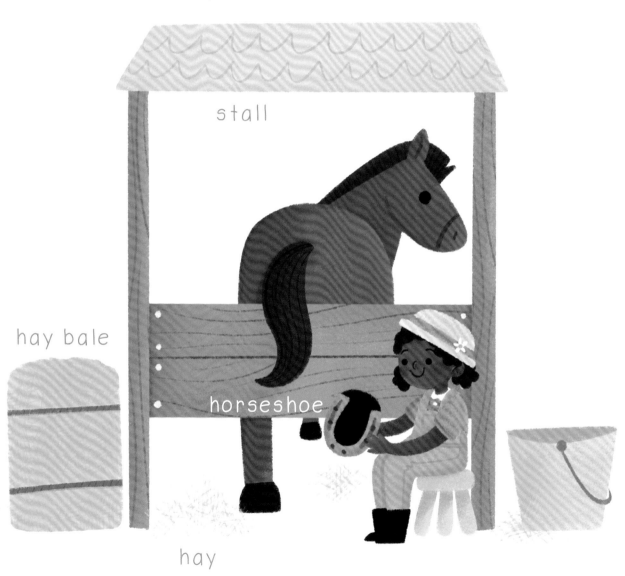

stall

hay bale

horseshoe

hay

Horses wear shoes to protect their hooves!
In the wild, a horse's hooves stay strong and
healthy on their own, but horses that live and
work on the farm need extra help. Horseshoes
can help horses safely walk on rough or slippery
surfaces.

mane

field

WHAT ELSE CAN FARM ANIMALS DO?

There is so much to learn about animals on the farm. Read more about each one here!

COW

Cows like to live in herds and can even have best friends.

Cows can swim.

Only females are called cows. Males are called bulls and babies are called calves.

CHICKEN

Chickens are one of the most common birds on Earth.

The red part on top of a chicken's head is called a comb.

Chickens can fly very short distances.

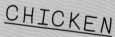

DUCK

Ducks have webbed feet to help them swim.

Ducks don't have any teeth.

Ducks are also called waterfowl.

PIG

A pig's nose is called a snout.

Some pigs have curly tails and some have straight tails.

Baby pigs are called piglets.

ROOSTER

Roosters have colorful tails and larger combs than hens.

Roosters are usually leaders of their flock.

Roosters have a claw-like body part called a spur on their leg.

CHICK

Baby chicks are born with an egg tooth to help them break out of their shell.

Not all baby chicks are yellow. Some can be black, brown, or even red.

SHEEP

Sheep like to live in groups called flocks.

Baby sheep are called lambs.

A sheep's wool coat is called a fleece.

DONKEY

Donkeys are very smart and very alert.

Donkeys make loud noises called braying.

Donkeys are very strong and can carry heavy loads.

HORSE

A male horse is called a stallion and a female horse is called a mare. A baby horse is called a foal.

Horses use their long tails to brush away flies and other insects.

DUCKLING

Baby ducklings aren't born with feathers. Like baby chicks, they are born with a soft coat called down.

Ducklings spend most of the day eating.